DATE DUE

APR 1 7 1997		
MAY 0 6 1997		
MAY 1 6 1997		
Nov 6 '02		
NO 15 '02		
FE 24 03		
NO 25 '03		
JA 13 '04		
AP 16 '04		
JA 27 '05		
OC 13 '05		
NO 01 '06		
NO 08 '06		
GAYLORD		PRINTED IN U S A

Military Aircraft Library
Navy Fighters

Military Aircraft Library
Navy Fighters

DR. DAVID BAKER

Rourke Enterprises, Inc.
Vero Beach, FL 32964

NAVY FIGHTERS

Developed from an original design by Northrop, the McDonnell Douglas FA-18 carrier-based fighter will remain with naval forces for at least the remainder of the century.

Library of Congress Cataloging-in-Publication Data
Baker, David, 1944-
  Navy fighters.

  (Military aircraft library)
  Includes index.
  Summary: Describes the history and design of different types of Navy fighters and their uses in combat.
  1. Fighter planes—Juvenile literature. 2. United States. Navy—Aviation—Juvenile literature.
  [1. Fighter planes. 2. United States. Navy—Aviation. 3. Airplanes, Military] I. Title. II. Series: Baker, David, 1944-   . Military planes.
  UG1242.F5B363 1987   358.4'3'0973   87-14144
  ISBN 0-86592-352-3

CONTENTS

Why Navy Fighters

When the United States went to war in 1941 to help defeat Nazi Germany and the Imperial Forces of the Japanese Empire, the country's armed forces had to fight many thousands of miles from home. Across the Pacific, Japan's naval forces were massing to attack ships of the United States Navy. They had already dealt a crippling blow to the Pacific fleet at Pearl Harbor in a surprise attack on December 7. The only way the United States could defeat her enemy was to carry planes across the sea and bring them within striking distance of enemy land, sea, and air forces. The response to this need was a massive building program for carriers and planes and the result was the largest floating air force anywhere.

One of the most outstanding aircraft programs was that put together to build the remarkable Hellcat. Designed and manufactured by Grumman, the F6F-1 Hellcat first flew in June, 1942. Grumman had already built the first plane with wings that not only folded over but back against the *fuselage* as well, doubling the number of planes that could be put aboard a single carrier. The Hellcat was a tough little fighter built for rugged, all-weather operation from a rolling deck. It could fly more than 1,000 miles, had a top speed of 376 MPH, and could lift 2,000 pounds of bombs, in addition to four machine guns or two cannon.

Hellcat production lasted for little more than three years. In that time, Grumman turned out 12,272 planes of this type, including 11,000 delivered in just two years and, in March 1945,

For more than forty years United States Navy carrier battle groups have been a formidable and awesome presence in every major ocean of the world.

One of the most successful navy planes to come out of World War II was the Vought Corsair, three of which are seen here.

605 in one month! The Hellcat destroyed more than 6,000 Japanese planes before the end of the war in 1945, but it proved time and again the value of a carrier-based task force.

After the war, development of jet-powered fighters brought a new look to carrier operations. The McDonnell FH-1 Phantom was the first jet to land on a carrier when Lt. Cdr. James Davidson touched down on the USS *Franklin D. Roosevelt,* 21 July, 1946. The FH-1 was soon obsolete, although it did equip the world's first shipboard jet fighter squadron, which converted to more advanced planes in 1950.

One type of fighter that bridged the transition to jets was the propeller-driven Vought Corsair fighter bomber, in production longer than any

Before the jets came along, propeller driven fighters like this Skyraider were able to land slow and steady on navy carrier decks.

other type before the jet-powered Phantom II. More than 12,500 Corsairs were built in the ten years from 1942 to 1952. This fighter-bomber saw service in the Korean War (1950-53), trucking 4,000 pound bomb loads into war at 240 MPH! Yet, although this performance appeared little better than that put out by fighters in the Second World War (1939-45), great changes were about to take place.

The need to get fighters on and off the carriers quickly and safely made naval designers look for innovative solutions. Planes were getting faster and heavier. The angled flight deck, adopted in 1952, seemed to be the only solution. With it, planes could land without hitting planes parked forward, and others could take off from steam-driven catapults.

Fighter plane weights were increasing by leaps and bounds. Hellcat weighed in at 14,000 pounds fully loaded. Grumman's jet-powered Panther and Cougar each weighed up to 20,000 pounds while McDonnell's Demon grossed 24,000 pounds. All these types entered service between 1950 and 1955, followed by the Vought Cutlass and Crusader in the second half of the 1950s. Weight now seemed to level off at around 32,000 pounds.

Performance had increased in line with weights, however. The FH-1 had a top speed of about 400 MPH. Within five years the Demon was almost 200 MPH faster, and by 1957 the Crusader was coming in to service with a top speed of nearly 1,100 MPH. In just ten years, speeds had nearly tripled. By the late 1950s, the

The introduction of jet fighters in the 1950s brought about a need for bigger carriers with more deck space. The plane shown here is a Grumman Cougar.

United States had all the elements of a major deterrent, a massive weapon system unlike anything else afloat.

Jet fighters got heavier during the 1950s and this Vought Crusader, at 32,000 lbs was about twice as heavy as the biggest World War II navy fighter.

The Heavyweights

With the introduction of jet fighter planes to U.S. Navy carrier duty, the ships themselves got bigger and stayed at sea longer.

Between 1941 and 1955, the U.S. Navy developed carrier air power to an unrivaled peak. No other country in the world possessed such naval air strength. It was important to the United States to have the proper tools to do an efficient job on behalf of her allies. The United States saw her powerful carrier battle groups as a very great instrument of peace.

In 1955 a new class of giant carriers was introduced with the USS *Forrestal*. Carriers of this type had a fully loaded displacement of 78,000 tons and helped pioneer operational use of the angled flight deck, first invented by the British. They were prototypes for the true supercarrier that came along in the early 1960s. First in the water was the USS *Enterprise*, combining the huge size of the *Forrestal* with a set of powerful nuclear reactors capable of operating for up to thirteen years. *Enterprise* and her sister ships could each carry 6,600 officers and men.

Directly in support of these giant ships, a new range of high-performance combat planes emerged during the 1960s. They all had the same characteristics: ruggedness, great structural strength, endurance, reliability, and two engines. Several hundred miles from shore with no other place to land, carrier planes are equipped with two engines to increase safety and insurance against failure. Combat planes are expensive, and while the pilot might survive a plunge in the sea, his aircraft certainly would not. Consequently, many navy planes get used on land, and some are purchased by the U.S. Air Force. Because they are not as strong as their seaborne counterparts, no land-based fighter has ever been sold to the navy.

Conflicting demands make the design of navy fighters complicated and designers face even more difficulties than they do when designing land-based fighters. While having exceptional strength to withstand countless heavy landings, navy fighters must be lighter than their air force equivalents. They must land more slowly so they can stop in a shorter distance, yet they must be able to carry large weapon loads. They must be as small as possible to give more space on deck, and they probably need folding wings to fit on the lifts that carry them down to hangars or the maintenance bays. In addition, they should resist salt and spray pouring over the deck from a heaving sea.

Space aboard a carrier is always at a premium and almost all navy planes must fold their wings to make room on deck for fighters taking off and landing.

Not many planes can match these requirements. One that did, however, became the best jet fighter ever made. Built by McDonnell Douglas and officially called the F4, it is best known simply as the Phantom and has achieved fame with many air forces. Designed around two very powerful afterburning *turbojets*, delivering a combined thrust of 34,000 pounds, it first flew in 1958. The Phantom weighed between 50,000 pounds and 60,000 pounds, depending on the version. Used by the navy as a fleet defense fighter, at first it had no gun and relied instead on four air-to-air missiles. Yet the rugged construction, powerful performance, and weight-lifting capacity of the Phantom made it an ideal candidate for external stores.

The Phantom was not in service long when the M61 multi-barrel gun was fitted under the nose and pylons were attached for Sparrow and Sidewinder missiles. Other stores, including bombs and reconnaissance pods, could be carried up to a total weight of 16,000 pounds. The Phantom has been adapted from an all-weather interceptor into a multi-role fighter for land or sea operation. It is in service with the air force and the marine corps and has been purchased by air forces in England, Iran, South Korea, Israel, West Germany, Australia, Spain, Japan, Greece, and Turkey.

When United States armed forces helped the government of South Vietnam against communist aggression from the north during the 1960s and early 1970s, the Phantom became the principle attack plane in Southeast Asia. In the air defense and ground attack role, its use provided a good example of how an exceptionally strong airframe for rugged carrier duty can be effective in the demanding arena of low-altitude combat. Buffeted by ground fire and turbulent air low down, the Phantom successfully came out of situations other fighters would not have survived. More than 5,200 were built, the largest number of jet fighter planes ever ordered from a manufacturer outside the Soviet Union.

Ground handling crews using small motor driven tugs maneuver planes for take-off and for storage.

One of the most famous post-war jet fighters to emerge for navy duty was the McDonnell Douglas F-4 Phantom seen here taking off.

The Phantom was the only navy fighter bought in large numbers by the Air Force and has served in many countries and several conflicts throughout the world.

A Modern
Navy Fighter

When looking for a modern, high performance, carrier-based combat interceptor, there is no better example than the U.S. Navy's F-14 Tomcat built by Grumman Aerospace. This plane makes use of almost every Navy fighter technology, with some that no other planes use. The Tomcat was designed in the late 1960s to provide the U.S. Navy with a partial replacement for the F-4 Phantom.

As early as 1957, the navy was becoming concerned that development of Soviet cruise missiles could pose a serious threat to carrier battle groups. The Phantom could only attack an enemy aircraft or slow-flying cruise missile at relatively short range, perhaps 20 miles at most. What was needed was a fighter able to attack threatening planes and air-launched missiles several hundred miles from the carriers using a missile system with a range of up to 100 miles.

The long range patrol duty aboard big navy carriers today is carried out by the Grumman F-14 Tomcat, two of which are seen here crossing the coast of California.

The Tomcat has wings that sweep back against the tail for high speed flight enabling it to reach more than Mach 2.

More than that, this fighter should also be able to attack several targets at the same time.

At first the U.S. Navy tried to adapt the General Dynamics F-111 then being built for the U.S. Air Force as a land-based fighter, but the F-111 was too heavy. In 1969, the U.S. Navy chose Grumman's F-14 design, and within two years the prototype had made its first flight. Although only a few years separated design of the F-111 and the F-14, the Navy fighter used more advanced technology and benefited from having been designed from the outset for carrier operations. This feature allowed engineers to build the Tomcat just as the Navy wanted it, without the compromise that would have made the F-111 a second-rate system for ship work.

Yet, like the F-111, the F-14 made use of the swing-wing design that allowed high-speed maneuvering in the air and slow speed handling for carrier landings. This design, called the *variable geometry wing,* was a ready-made solution for problems associated with navy fighter design. Because navy fighters had grown heavy (the Phantom weighed in at a maximum 58,000 pounds), the landing speeds had also gone up to generate sufficient lift. The F-14 would weigh up to 72,000 pounds so a radical solution was necessary. Heavy aircraft are big and cannot maneuver as well as lighter, smaller, planes. Some sort of compromise was essential.

To land a fighter on a rolling carrier in the limited length of a flight deck, the plane's speed

For landing, or low speed maneuvering, the Tomcat pivots its wings to the forward position giving it good lift and control characteristics.

must be low. But in combat, both range and high speed are necessary. To get both capabilities on the same aircraft, the wing would have to be able to be virtually redesigned in flight. The swing-wing did just that, and it enabled the F-14 to adapt to many different flying needs. There was another benefit to the swing-wing. Wings that fold tight against the body of the plane make room for more aircraft on deck.

Another reason for designing the wing to swivel around from a fully swept to a fully extended position is to help the pilot during close-in combat. Unlike any other swing-wing aircraft, the Tomcat has small glove vanes which automatically help the air move properly over the swept wing. These vanes are connected to an automatic control system rather like a computer, which constantly moves the wings in and out without the pilot having to manually operate them. Left to concentrate on out-maneuvering his opponent, the pilot lets the plane automatically set its own wing position for the

best possible angle of sweep. This close-in combat is still very important. Navy and Air Force pilots cannot rely on more than one-third to one-half of their missiles hitting enemy aircraft.

With a total thrust of up to 41,800 pounds from two powerful Pratt & Whitney engines, the Tomcat is capable of *Mach* 2.34, or 1,564 MPH. With a full load of fuel the F-14 has a maximum range of 2,000 miles. It carries either Sidewinder or Sparrow missiles for attacking at close range or up to six Phoenix missiles for targets more than 100 miles away. It also carries a rotary cannon for close-in combat and with its agile twisting and turning can out-perform most potentially hostile planes in the air today. The Tomcat is continually being improved upon, and although it entered service as early as 1972, this fighter will continue to provide long range air defense for U.S. carrier battle groups wherever they are called upon to operate well into the twenty-first century.

Each carrier operates two Tomcat squadrons, about twenty-four planes, for patrolling the ocean several hundred miles away from the battle group.

The Tomcat's folding wings come in handy where space is at a premium, as in this view of a hangar below decks.

Electronic Phoenix

Navy Tomcats are built to go after the difficult targets, long range bombers, low-flying cruise missiles and high-flying escort fighters. They must get in close for the occasional dog-fight and protect carriers against attack. If one nuclear-tipped cruise missile gets through, the Tomcat has no place to go back to. Unlike land fighters, navy pilots can rarely divert to another air base. The reason the task force commander wants Tomcat to do its job is that he probably has about 40 attack planes to fly on and off the flight deck. The F-14's job is to protect that valuable piece of real estate.

Tomcat does that job with the aid of some of the world's most sophisticated electronics, radar, and missile systems. The object is always to stay ahead of the threat. Only in that way can F-14s keep their guns muzzled and peace intact. If an enemy believes he can overwhelm defense forces and gain air superiority, he may be tempt-

The Tomcat's cockpit is roomy and a lot more comfortable than many land based fighters, as is apparent in this view of the front seat.

ed to try to do so. Therefore, the enemy must be kept at bay, away from vulnerable targets like ships at sea. So Tomcat must protect surface vessels that have no planes to defend them and provide a shield against missiles and enemy aircraft.

The Tomcat faces these threats with the most advanced weapon system in the world. Called the AWG-9 radar weapon control system, it works in conjunction with the AIM-54 Phoenix missile, both built by Hughes. The carrier threat seemed daunting. Before the existence of Tomcat, a pilot going after an attack plane that had launched a cruise missile had to decide whether to go for the aircraft (which may have more cruise weapons) or the missile. With Tomcat, he can go after both at the same time. As we shall see in the next two sections, cruise weapons move relatively slowly to their targets but may carry large nuclear charges.

Tomcat fighter pilots rely on their rear seat crew members to operate the weapon systems and navigation equipment.

The Tomcat is the only plane that can use the long range Phoenix missile to shoot down targets more than one hundred miles away at heights between sea level and 100,000 feet. This Tomcat has the full load of six Phoenix missiles on board.

Phoenix and the AWG-9 radar is still the only weapon system in existence that can go after aerial targets farther than 100 miles away, tracking up to 24 separate targets at the same time, six of which can be attacked simultaneously. In theory, two squadrons of 12 Tomcats each could fend off 144 incoming attack planes, each equipped with two missiles, any one of which could sink the carrier. In reality, it would hardly ever work out like that. Instead, the enemy would probably throw up a combination of widely different threats. In several simulated exercises of this type, F-14s have repeatedly succeeded at doing what in actual combat would result in a perfect interception.

A typical interception begins when the AWG-9's 36-inch antenna, mounted inside the plane's nose, identifies a potential target. The weapons officer in the rear seat switches to the Single Target Track mode. This locks the antenna to a single target up to 80 miles away. The missile can be fired at a range of 62 miles. Before firing, the weapons officer will use a television camera in front of the back seat to give him a magnified picture of the aircraft. This lets him view the target and confirm whether it is friend or foe. Even at 100 miles, he could identify a large plane like the Boeing 747 Jumbo Jet. In what is called the Pulse Doppler Search Mode, targets up to 125 miles away can be located and tracked. As the plane closes on the targets ahead, the Track While Scan computer program allows several missiles to be launched simultaneously.

The AWG-9 itself weighs around 1,235 pounds and each set costs more than $2.2 million. It can process 550,000 calculations a second, beating the AP101 computers in the NASA shuttle! Its radar has twenty times more power output than the Phantom and almost twice that of the land-based F-15. It can burn through jamming signals from enemy planes and has an excellent record of reliability. The Phoenix missile has been successfully fired against a wide variety of simulated targets, and there is no doubt that it works very well. In one test, an F-14 attacked a

simulated Mig-25 Foxbat at Mach 2.7 and 80,000 feet and then a Mach 1.5 bomber at 50,000 feet. Yet another struck down a simulated, *subsonic,* anti-ship missile 50 feet above the waves. In one attack a single Phoenix soared to a height of almost 104,000 feet before diving to its target 127 miles away.

Although on test, this Tomcat fires its Phoenix missiles as if in response to an incoming airborne threat.

In a major conflict the kind of planes the Tomcats would be up against include this Mig-25 Foxbat equipped with anti-aircraft missiles.

Fighter Weapons

Combat weapons fall into three main categories: air-to-air missiles, air-to-surface missiles, and guns. Dog-fights and close-in combat between fast planes using gun or cannon are getting less and less likely with each passing year. There is almost no situation today where navy fighters get that close to the enemy. Air-to-air missiles (AAMs), however, are increasingly the chosen mode of turning back attacking aircraft. These fall into three general classifications: heat-seeking, semi-active radar, and fully-active radar.

An AAM that uses heat-seeking sensors is equipped with sensitive equipment scanning changes in temperature within a limited *arc*. As the missile flies, the sensors "see" hot targets like engine exhausts in the general direction the missile is launched. Special filters and electronics protect the missile from heading off in the direction of the sun! Heat-seeking AAMs are limited, however, in that anything hotter than the enemy plane's exhaust plume will cause the missile to switch targets. Some planes carry flares ejected in the path of the incoming missile to fool the missile's *infrared* sensors.

The most common AAMs in use with navy planes are the short-range AIM-9 Sidewinder and the long-range AIM-7 Sparrow. These missiles have been around for several decades and are used by many air forces around the world. Nearly 200,000 Sidewinders have been built so far, and production lines have been set up in Europe and Japan. More than 80,000 are currently in use. Some versions of the AIM-9 are used only in the United States. Over the years, improvements to the missile's range have increased its radius of action from around 2 miles in early versions to about 11 miles in the latest versions. Sidewinder is a heat-seeker, equipped

This Tomcat is equipped with Sparrow and Sidewinder missiles for dogfighting or short range attack out to a distance of about twenty miles.

Tomcat can carry Phoenix (white missiles in the center), Sparrow (larger missiles on inboard pylons), or Sidewinder (outer pylons) to combat air threats.

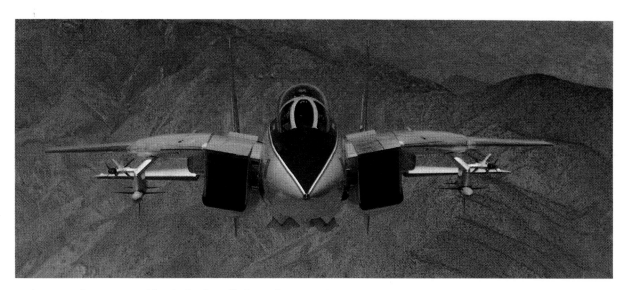

The AIM-9L Sidewinder installed on this Intruder is typical of pylon mountings for navy planes using this weapon.

with tiny infrared sensors that work through guidance electronics to control small fins on the body of the missile.

Sparrow is a semi-active radar homing missile. It was developed at a time when the biggest threat came from subsonic bombers cruising at high altitude. When used against Russian-built jets in Southeast Asia during the Vietnam conflict, it was a flop. All 21 Sparrows that were fired at Mig fighters during one engagement failed to hit their targets. The missile was rapidly redesigned, and new modified versions emerged. Today, Sparrow is a formidable weapon, limited only by the way it operates.

Because Sparrow is a semi-active radar missile, the plane that launches it must keep its own radar locked on the target. In the case of the F-14, this means that the target must be kept within a 65-degree cone of the plane's nose, where the antenna is located. As the missile flies to its target, it tracks signals put out by the F-14,

Anti-aircraft missiles are just a part of the load carried by most navy planes. The missile in the center with fins is the long range AIM-7 Sparrow.

reflected back from the plane it is attacking. In order to give the Sparrow a reflected beam, the F-14 must "illuminate" the target with radar signals that the attacking aircraft would detect. The pilot of that plane might then fire off a heat-seeking missile in return, destroying the F-14 seconds after he was hit and destroyed by the Sparrow.

Sparrow normally has a range of about 30 miles, but this range increases to more than 40 miles when used with the F-14. The greater range is due to the Tomcat's powerful AWG-9 radar, designed primarily for the Phoenix missile. This very long-range weapon carries an active radar, the only sensible concept for attacking targets up to 100 miles off. For targets less than 13 miles distant, the internal radar instantly locks on the enemy plane and Phoenix guides itself without further help from the F-14. For long-range attack, the missile is launched from the F-14 (the only plane equipped to carry Phoenix) in the general direction of the target. For most of the way the missile flies a pre-set course on autopilot. Within a calculated distance to the target it switches to active mode, searches for the target, locks on, and steers itself to a direct hit, destroying the target with a 132-pound high explosive charge.

Tomcat pilots rarely have to flex their muscles in anger, but practice regularly to be ready in case they are needed.

Threats
to Survival

In recent years the Soviet navy has been growing and additions to the Russian fleet include these new aircraft carriers.

Fighter planes exist to protect resources vital in time of war. Navy fighters must operate under arduous conditions and deter threatening forces from attack. The aircraft carrier supports large numbers of planes, only a portion of which are there to protect the battle group. Carriers operate in battle groups because they serve as floating airfields and sometimes need additional seaborne resources to back up a military operation. For instance, cruisers might be needed to bombard surface installations, or destroyers might be called upon to fend off enemy ships in the area. Submarines patrol beneath the surface to protect the carrier force from underwater attack. The fighters on the carrier keep control of airspace around the fleet.

The free movement of United States shipping across international waters could be threatened in several ways. By far the most versatile threat would come from long-range bombers, at most only a few hours away from Atlantic or Pacific Ocean sea forces. In-flight refueling would extend the bomber's range and also allow it the option of flying a long, circuitous route to its target, thereby avoiding detection for as long as possible. The carrier force can do very little to avoid detection. In fact its movements are accurately recorded on a continual basis by potentially hostile forces.

United States carrier battle groups are frequently "inspected" by long-range Soviet maritime reconnaissance planes. The Russian navy operates about 105 planes for this job, divided equally among three types. The Tu-95 Bear is a four engined *turboprop* aircraft capable of an unrefueled range of 5,150 miles and can remain in the air for up to 28 hours at a constant speed of 400 MPH. Although faster by about 100 MPH, the twin turbojet Tu-16 Badger has much less range. The Tu-22 Blinder is better on range and faster too, capable of a Mach 1.5 dash or 550 MPH at sea level.

The Soviet navy also operates 240 Badgers and 35 Blinders in the bombing role, along with 120 Backfire B planes posing a serious threat to surface vessels. Each carries one or more cruise

United States carrier forces are under continual threat from lurking submarines of the type shown here.

From the air, one of the main threats to the carriers themselves would come from cruise missiles launched from long range bombers like this Backfire.

Backfires attacking naval forces would be escorted part of the way by Soviet air defense fighters as depicted in this artist's illustration.

A Tomcat trails a Soviet Bear bomber and escorts it away.

missiles powered by rocket or turbojet engines. Released some distance from their targets, cruise missiles fly at high or low altitude, depending on type. They are suitable targets in themselves, and F-14 Tomcats would try to shoot them down before they reached the ships against which they had been targeted.

The Backfire has a top speed of 1,265 MPH and represents a considerable improvement on earlier types of bombers like the Blinder, from which it was developed. Like its predecessor, the Backfire can carry one or two AS-4 Kitchen cruise missiles. With a range exceeding 300 miles, the Kitchen has a *1-megaton* nuclear warhead and can cruise at Mach 3. In one application, it could detonate its nuclear charge to destroy the carrier by blast, and the resulting tidal wave would sink remaining ships. The Backfire B has a combat radius of up to 2,600 miles. Although this radius is not enough to threaten cities in the United States, it is sufficient to pose a serious threat in the Atlantic and Pacific Oceans. Most Backfires are based in sup-

port of the Soviet Pacific Fleet.

A successor to Backfire is Blackjack, which has been in development since the mid-1970s. It first became operational in 1987 and, like the Backfire, has a variable geometry wing allowing it to adapt to several different operational roles. One of these roles will be to serve as a maritime reconnaissance and strike plane. Blackjack has a maximum speed of 1,380 MPH and an operational radius of 4,540 miles. It has four immense *augmented turbofan engines* that deliver a maximum combined thrust of 200,000 pounds.

Threats like these bring heavy responsibility to the patrolling fighters that keep watch on the carrier battle group's outer defenses. With several tiered layers in ever widening circles out from the carrier and its escort vessels to far beyond the horizon, the F-14s watch the distant threats while other shorter-range planes patrol closer in. A modern nuclear-powered carrier will usually carry about 24 Tomcats to defend airspace several hundred miles around the battle group.

Dual Roles

Space is at a premium on a tightly packed carrier with planes taking off from the steam-driven catapults, coming in to a screeching stop along the angled flight deck, going up and down on lifts between maintenance bays, and being wheeled about getting ready for a mission. It is not surprising that the navy sometimes needs its planes to do two or three different jobs at different times.

Most navy fighters are readily transformed into attack planes because they are built to be tough and strong. This makes them ideal for holding external stores like rockets, bombs, and extra fuel tanks to extend the range. Only one aircraft can be found aboard a carrier today that lives the life of a fighter and nothing else: the F-14 Tomcat. It is left to do its job of patrolling the outer defenses and fending off incoming attack because it is almost uniquely suited to that role. Other planes do not have the privilege of being assigned a single duty. They are there to do the job the carrier exists for: to deter conflict and show a United States presence in faraway places.

One of the most successful light to medium attack planes is the McDonnell Douglas A-4 Skyhawk.

The Skyhawk has been used many times in action and is only now being replaced by many years of service.

One of the first and most adaptable dual-role navy fighters of the jet age was the McDonnell Douglas A4 Skyhawk. In 1952 the navy put out a specification that sought a light carrier-based attack plane to replace the propeller-driven Skyraider. Douglas designer Ed Heinemann took up the challenge of what many considered to be an impossible goal: a plane that had a top speed of 500 MPH, a range of 345 miles with a 2,000-pound warload, and a maximum weight of less than 30,000 pounds. Heinemann beat that goal. He produced a plane capable of 673 MPH and a combat radius of 460 miles with a maximum warload of 9,155 pounds. The maximum weight never grew beyond 24,000 pounds. Some land-based planes, however, did eventually weigh 27,000 pounds.

The Skyhawk first flew in 1954 and entered production for the U.S. Navy that year. This plane remained in production for 25 years, longer than any other combat plane. Skyhawk is a compact machine capable of rugged operation, and yet it is so small that it is one of the few navy planes with non-folding wings. Its wingspan is just 27 feet, 6 inches, 11 feet less than the folded span of an F-14 and equal to the total span of an F4 Phantom. The cockpit is positioned high above the nose for good visibility, and the landing gear is high, permitting good clearance for wing stores.

As an attack plane, the Skyhawk saw extensive service with the navy in Vietnam. It can

carry Sidewinder short-range missiles on under-wing pylons in addition to a pair of cannon fitted in the *wing root* as standard armament. A wide range of bombs and rockets can be installed on the Skyhawk. It has been exported to Argentina, Australia, Israel, New Zealand, Singapore, Kuwait, Indonesia, and Malaysia. Some 2,960 Skyhawks have been built, including a two-seat training version, the TA-4. Designed to partially replace costly F-14 Tomcat air superiority fighters, the McDonnell Douglas F/A-18 Hornet has emerged as a versatile strike plane and defense, protecting the fleet close in against

The F-18 Hornet, seen here amid steam generated by the catapult, has been sold to several countries as a land fighter.

multi-role fighter, another dual mission aircraft. It was based heavily on the Northrop YF-17 that failed to win the competition for a lightweight, land-based, fighter won by General Dynamics with the F-16. The Hornet never did replace any Tomcats, but it added an inner layer of carrier

The design of the Hornet indicates the essential features of a navy fighter, including an added measure of safety assured by the two engines, a rugged and compact airframe, and advanced navigation and radar gear with the nose-mounted antenna.

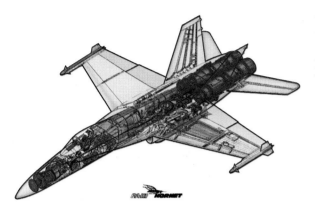

intruders that got through the outer lines.

Because it is equally at home in a dog-fight, scrapping with a persistent enemy fighter, or carrying up to 17,000 lb of rockets and bombs on a strike mission, the Hornet epitomizes the dual role. It is fast, with a top speed around 1,200 MPH, and it can carry a full weapon load on a round trip of more than 1,000 miles. Most operations of this type would take place against land targets and sometimes in support of marine corps operations. In fact, the marines have ordered Hornets for themselves. In addition, Hornet has been sold to Australia, Canada, and Spain.

The Hornet is used for defense of the inner regions around a carrier battle group and for light to medium attack duties on sea and land targets.

The
Heavy Punch

The Douglas Skywarrior had a range of 1,000 miles and was used as a carrier based nuclear strike bomber.

Traditionally, carriers have packed a heavy punch. They have had to. Far from the United States, possibly surrounded by unfriendly countries, the stabilizing presence of a naval task force has more than once deterred aggression. They are a deterrent because the potential enemy believes that the carrier's planes can deliver such a massive blow it is not worth his while to attack. Today, the carrier is responsible for helping allies and friendly countries fend off an unprovoked strike. It is there to provide a force capable of keeping the peace or backing up a combined land, sea, and air force attack if hostilities do break out.

The carrier's role has not always been the same as it is now. For many years into the age of nuclear weapons after the Second World War, it was part of the United States' strategic deterrent. Carrier-based planes were available, ready to carry atomic weapons to attack

military targets very far away. By the 1970s, that role had been replaced by one similar to an international policing mission. Although carriers have nuclear weapons on board, these weapons would only be used in battles on land between military forces. Because of this, they are called *tactical battlefield nuclear weapons*.

Strategic forces are those held back as an ultimate deterrent. Large nuclear warheads are now carried by long-range missiles and by heavy bombers based in the United States. They are part of a strategy based on this belief: only if a potential enemy really believes he cannot survive nuclear retaliation will he stop before escalating what might be a minor conflict into a war involving many countries. When the navy carrier was part of the strategic deterrent, special planes were needed to carry atomic bombs over great distances. The first of these was the Douglas Skywarrior with a range of

1,000 miles and a maximum speed of 610 MPH. The first squadron became operational in 1956. The presence of these planes on the flight decks of carriers in the Mediterranean and the Pacific did much to bring home the reality of United States military capability.

The strategic nuclear role did not last long and eventually gave way to an emphasis on tactical bombing in support of limited wars. The

The Rockwell Vigilante replaced the Douglas nuclear bomber in the long range attack role until it was retired in the 1970s.

With afterburners at full bore, this dramatic shot of a Vigilante climbing off the carrier deck emphasizes its enormous (20 ton) weight.

The mainstay of light strike duty in the carrier battle group today, this Grumman A-6 Intruder has just landed on the flight deck.

transition period was bridged by three aircraft, all of which joined the navy within a four year period. The last of the nuclear bombers was the Rockwell A-5 Vigilante. It crammed more high technology into its huge airframe than any other aircraft of its day. It was big, with a length of 76 feet, a wing span of 53 feet, and a maximum weight of 80,000 pounds. Nevertheless, it could lift an atomic warload, had a range of 3,200 miles and a top speed of 1,385 MPH, more than twice the speed of sound. Vigilante joined the navy in 1962. One year later, the Grumman Intruder arrived, first of a tough new breed.

Grumman had built navy planes since 1931. They were tough and they were reliable. So was the Intruder, designed to expand the role of the A4 Skyhawk as a punchy, all-weather, attack plane capable of pin-point bombing on land targets. It represented lessons from the Korean War (1950-53) and firmly set the role of the carrier on track as a tactical support force. Very soon, the Intruder replaced the Vigilante as a nuclear bomber, and several Vigilantes were converted to the reconnaissance role. With its enormous range, the Vigilante did well in that capacity. The A-6 Intruder works best in support of on-shore activities usually involving marines. It is a very good back-up weapon for an assault role or for dropping bombs very accurately, where the enemy may be close to friendly troops. The Intruder will be more fully described in the next section with marine aviation.

Within three years of Intruder joining the carriers in 1963, the navy took delivery of the Corsair II built by Vought. The Corsair was the second of two attack planes that would serve as the backbone of naval air strike power for many years. Corsair was adapted from the Crusader supersonic fighter. It became a subsonic long range machine capable of carrying a weapon load of up to 20,000 pounds. With full tanks it has a strike radius of more than 700 miles and extends to greater range a similar role carried out by the much smaller Skyhawk. It is now being gradually replaced by the F/A-18 Hornet, a truly diverse new plane.

For many years the carrier's medium-weight punch on land targets has been the responsibility of the Vought Corsair, a rugged and capable plane now being replaced by the Hornet.

Attack

The Grumman Intruder emerged after the Korean War, where it was felt a heavier and harder-hitting equivalent of the successful little Skyhawk was necessary. Both navy and marine flyers saw the need for an all-weather attack plane able to hit hard in fog, rain, mist, or snow and in heavy fire from the enemy. The *prototype* flew in 1960, and it entered service three years later. It has no particular need to fly fast, so its designers concentrated instead on providing good stability and a capacity to make very ac-

curate bombing runs. Accuracy is important, because marines on the ground will ask the plane to hit targets very close to where they are hiding. They have to trust the pilot not to hit them too, so the aircraft must be capable of precision bombing at the first attempt. A strike plane that has to go around for another try might not survive the second run-in.

On a typical attack mission at night and in bad weather, the two Intruder crewmen sit comfortably side by side, illuminated by reflected light from numerous instruments and dials. The pilot sits on the left and the bombardier/navigator on the right. Intruder would fly just 200 feet above the sea at about 600 MPH, not fast by today's

A squadron of Intruders head for an inland target under the protection of electronic surveillance from carrier based early warning planes.

Dropping to low altitude, an Intruder enters enemy air space and makes ready for its final run to the target.

standards. It might take an hour for the plane to fly from the carrier where it took off to the general area of the target.

The crew would be wearing night-vision goggles to help them see better in the dark. These are like small binoculars attached to their helmets. As they look through them they get much the same view they would with the unaided eye at dusk. Red colors are enhanced by the goggles, so all lights inside the cockpit are blue-green instead of the usual dull red. This prevents the goggles from giving the wearer a brighter view of the plane's interior.

To further help the pilot see ahead in the dark, a big section of the canopy carries a projected image generated by a special sensor. Called the Forward Looking Infrared Radar, or Flir, it uses infrared sensors to show the pilot the view in front, projected on the canopy in what is called a "head-up" display, or HUD. Although the plane's course may be programmed by a computer-driven guidance system, the pilot needs to "see" the way ahead through the HUD-generated image. With his goggles on he can get a feel for the terrain outside.

For example, during a night attack mission, the computer-controlled approach path might require the plane to fly low through a valley with

steeply rising walls. In the cockpit, the pilot's Flir would depict his flight path and the features ahead, but the goggles would make him aware of the valley walls on either side. This restores the awareness of hills, valleys, and trees outside, taken away from the pilot's natural vision by darkness or foul weather.

Within about 100 miles of the enemy coast the Intruder increases its height above the sea to get a radar image of the terrain ahead. As the pilot conducts the brief pop-up maneuver, his

Intruder pilots wear these special binoculars to help them see better in the dark and define visual targets out the window.

A special display monitor enables the pilot to read the instrumentation without taking his eyes off the view in front.

Its mission over, an Intruder comes back to the carrier.

navigator operates the radar which projects a near-perfect HUD view on the canopy. The navigator compares this with a moving map display which shows precisely where the plane is headed. It might be the mouth of a river flanked by farmland that rises to steep foothills. Down again just 200 feet above the sea, Intruder races on undetected. Other electronic sensors identify the target, a large tender, or warship, floating at anchor on moorings near the river mouth.

Less than a minute away from the target, another Flir system located under the plane's nose rolls around seeking the tender. It finds it and projects an image to the bombardier/navigator. He moves a computer-generated cross on his TV screen over the target image and sets up the missile electronics to lock on. The bombardier now switches on a thin beam of invisible laser light and points it at the target. The flir scanner maintains its lock on the target even as the Intruder is taking violent evasive action to escape ground fire. The missile is released and sensors in its nose follow the laser beam until it strikes the target.

Moving now to the other Flir system the pilot banks hard over 90 degrees to escape. To get back, perhaps he will fly fast up a valley floor flanked by steep walls. Although dark outside, the pilot will "see" the rugged terrain on his head-up image and sense the steep walls through his night-vision goggles. Safely away, he crosses the coast and begins the return journey.

The Task Force

The United States Navy operates fourteen aircraft carriers. Most are powered by giant turbine engines giving a top speed of up to 33 *knots*, which is 38 MPH. All but two are between 1,040 feet and 1,070 feet in length with a maximum width at the broadest section across the flight deck of up to 268 feet. Only two carriers of the Midway class are smaller, with a length of 980 feet. All conventional carriers *displace* between 64,000 tons and 82,000 tons. A typical carrier of this type would carry a ship crew of 2,000 officers and men with an additional 2,150 designated air crew. The oldest vessels, the two carriers of the Midway class, were built between 1945 and 1947. The others are much more modern, the most recent being *commissioned*, or put into use in 1968.

The carrier battle group is equipped with several squadrons of planes designed to protect the ships, deter attack from naval and air threats, and strike, when called upon, land targets several hundred miles away.

Five United States carriers are in a class of their own. They are powered by pressurized-water-cooled nuclear reactors driving four geared turbines. Each ship is about 1,100 feet in length and 250 feet across the beam, displacing up to 91,400 tons and capable of more than 30 knots (34 MPH). A big advantage with nuclear-powered carriers lies in the infrequent refuelings needed to re-charge the nuclear reactors with uranium cores. Super-carriers of the *Nimitz* and *Enterprise* class refuel only once every thirteen years. Moreover, the space vacated by ships fuel tanks carried in conventional carriers allows 50 percent more aviation fuel for the planes.

Completed in 1961, *Enterprise* was the first nuclear-powered carrier. It was followed by the *Nimitz*, the *Dwight D. Eisenhower*, the *Carl Vinson*, and the *Theodore Roosevelt*, the most recent of which was completed in 1986. Together these carriers represent a massive investment. With the exception of the *Enterprise*, with a complement of 4,900, each one carries 6,300 officers and men, of which 3,000 are air crew. Improvements in carriers built after the *Enterprise* added an extra 20 percent aviation fuel due to better design below deck. A sixth nuclear carrier will join the fleet in 1990 and bring to fifteen

Moving planes around on the carrier deck is a full time job for deck crews that must keep the carrier ever ready for war.

the total United States carrier force.

Many improvements in design have made life aboard the "flat-tops," as they are called, pleasant compared with that aboard carriers forty and fifty years ago. Yet the demands on men and equipment has not stopped. In fact, it has risen. With many more planes, most of which are high-performance jets, responsibilities have never

Approximately 2,500 ships' personnel are employed in support of the several squadrons stored in the hangars or on the flight deck.

With fuel, ammunition and bombs, ground crews must handle a continual flow of equipment from the hangars and stores up to the flight deck.

been greater. A typical mix of planes would include two F-14 Tomcat fighter squadrons totaling 24 aircraft. Three would be for reconnaissance, and the remaining 21 would be operating in the fleet defense role. Some carriers still use Phantoms instead of Tomcats.

The strike role would be met with two light attack squadrons of 24 Hornets or Corsairs and one medium attack squadron with 10 Intruders. Anti-submarine defense would support a squadron of 10 S-3A Viking fixed-wing aircraft and a squadron of 6 helicopters. Four Grumman Prowlers would conduct electronic countermeasure, a method of confusing an enemy attack by jamming his radar, and early warning of approaching planes would be carried out by four Grumman Hawkeyes. Finally, four modified Intruders, called KA-6D, would serve as in-flight refueling tankers.

Carriers can be on patrol for several months at a time, and although no effort is spared to make life comfortable, navy fliers are constantly ready to go into action at a moment's notice. The role of the navy fighter pilot has become more important as new and advanced technology provides many more countries with efficient combat weapons. In irresponsible hands, these weapons can become very effective against ships as big as a modern carrier. The fighter pilots who protect the carrier task force do so in the knowledge that frequently the lives of up to 6,000 men depend on their ability to stop an attack at its source.

Ever ready to go, this Corsair is about to be hurled into the air by the force of a steam propelled catapult.

ABBREVIATIONS

AAM   Air-to-Air Missile

FLIR   Forward Looking Infrared Radar

HUD   "Head-Up" Display

GLOSSARY

Arc
Something curved in shape or a section of an unbroken curved line. In this context, a sensor scanning back and forth along a section (arc) of a circle.

Augmented turbofan engine
A jet engine with circular compressors to increase the volume of air taken in through the front, with burners behind the combustion chamber to give additional energy to the exhausted gases by reigniting them as they leave the nozzle.

Commissioned
The date upon which an active ship is deemed to be seaworthy and capable of military activity.

Displacement
The weight or volume of water displaced by a floating or submerged boat.

Fuselage
The main body of an airplane to which are attached the wings and tail sections.

Infrared
The part of the electromagnetic spectrum with a longer wavelength than light but a shorter wavelength than radio waves. Like radio waves, infrared radiation cannot be seen with the unaided human eye.

Knots
The speed of an object measured in nautical miles per hour. A nautical mile has just over 6,076 feet compared to a statute mile which has 5,280 feet. Therefore, 10 nautical MPH (knots) is equal to 11.5 static MPH (usually just expressed as 11.5 MPH).

Mach
Mach 1, or unity, is the speed of sound: 760 MPH at sea level, decreasing to 660 MPH at a height of 36,000 feet. Mach 2.2 is equivalent to a speed of 1,672 MPH at sea level or 1,452 MPH above 36,000 feet.

Megaton
In the context of rating the explosive yield of a nuclear weapon, 1 megaton (or MT) would be equivalent to the explosive yield of one million tons of TNT.

Prototype
Defined as an original model upon which copies are based, usually regarded in aviation as the first flying airplane of a specific design.

Subsonic
Any speed below the speed of sound, which is about 760 MPH at sea level or about 660 MPH at 36,000 feet and above.

Tactical battlefield nuclear weapons
Nuclear weapons that are designed to be used on a battlefield to stop an advancing army, tanks, or other military equipment, but not weapons which are designed to attack towns, cities, or travel intercontinental distances.

Turbojet engine
A pure jet engine that reignites the burnt fuel-air mixture but without compressor blades in front.

Turboprop engine
A turbofan engine that compresses air taken in through an inlet, burns fuel in a combustion chamber, and drives a turbine connected to a shaft which runs along the length of the engine to a propeller at the front. Additional thrust is obtained by discharged exhaust gases out the nozzle.

Variable-geometry
A means by which the shape of an airplane wing can be changed in flight by attaching the wing to a pivot where it joins the main body (fuselage) so it can be swiveled to any position. This wing design is also called the swing-wing.

Wing root
The place on a plane where the wing joins the main body, or fuselage.

INDEX

Page references in *italics* indicate photographs or illustrations.